Giants Crossing

Giants Crossing

Poems by

Hilary Biehl

© 2025 Hilary Biehl. All rights reserved.
This material may not be reproduced in any form, published,
reprinted, recorded, performed, broadcast,
rewritten or redistributed without
the explicit permission of Hilary Biehl.
All such actions are strictly prohibited by law.

Cover design by Shay Culligan
Cover image by Sebastian Hemetsberger on Unsplash
Author photo by Kiara Miller

ISBN: 978-1-63980-815-1
Library of Congress Control Number: 2025949420

Kelsay Books
502 South 1040 East, A-119
American Fork, Utah 84003
Kelsaybooks.com

Acknowledgments

Thank you to the following publications, in which versions of these poems previously appeared:

Able Muse: "Exposure," "Figure Drawing"

Autumn Sky Poetry Daily: "Poem Illuminated by a Crow"

Better Than Starbucks: "Giants Crossing"

Blue Unicorn: "First Fishing Trip," "On Rising"

The Lyric: "After Hail," "The Fairy Path," "A Grasshopper"

Mezzo Cammin: "Bigfoot," "The Opposite of Aging"

The Orchards Poetry Journal: "Inventory of a Shop in Berkeley," "Nestlings"

Pulsebeat Poetry Journal: "The Leaf Blower," "For a Neighbor," "Things Done and Left Undone," "Without a Pause"

The Road Not Taken: "The Drive," "Her Broad-Brimmed Hat," "Visiting Switzerland at Seventeen"

THINK: "A Barbary Lion," "Faux Pas"

Contents

The Jackalope	13
Exposure	14
Cracks	15
Child Carrying a Dandelion	16
A Grasshopper	17
Wide-Angle	18
The Fairy Path	19
Visiting Switzerland at Seventeen	21
A Fairy Story	22
Mountain Wildflowers	24
Green People	25
An Apprehension	26
Inventory of a Shop in Berkeley	27
The Drive	28
Childproofing	29
Sticks	30
Fiber Arts	31
STAT	33
Reading Skin	34
Without a Pause	35
Fall	36
Out of Proportion	37
Giants Crossing	38
A Barbary Lion	39
Limbo	40
The Leaf Blower	41
Bigfoot	42
Unbecoming	43
Things Done and Left Undone	44
With the Current	46
For a Neighbor	47
Renovation	48

Old Cars	49
Harpies	50
The Bath	51
Poem Illuminated by a Crow	52
Sanctuary	53
Knitting Lesson	54
Inspiration	55
Adamantine	56
Her Broad-Brimmed Hat	57
Reading Hart Crane in the School Parking Lot	58
A Few Minor Poets	59
The Muse	60
Figure Drawing	61
The Female Form	62
Faux Pas	64
The Opposite of Aging	65
On Rising	66
In the Giants' Cottage	67
Emily and Blake	68
For Sergei Prokofiev	69
A Dream	70
Assisting the Day	71
Mildred	72
After Hail	73
Puddle Gazing	74
Nestlings	75
First Fishing Trip	76

The Jackalope

He shows us where they saw the jackalope.
Of course, it's just a row of houses now,
with driveways, sidewalks. He remembers how
wild cacti used to bloom, there, on that slope.
The tang of junipers. A flash of taupe
with antlers. And our mother nods, her brow
textured with memory, but won't allow
us to explore. We push the envelope
a little, wandering up the road where she
once tracked coyote footprints in the snow.
A fence stands in our way. "We're strangers here,"
she whispers, but we see it suddenly,
behind a trash can, bound and disappear.
"Look, Grandpa, look!" He takes our hands. "Let's go."

Exposure

Trees, stained black by snowmelt, lift the ghost
of foliage towards a gently shaken sky,
so spare and skeletal that every nest
is known. Just out of sight, birds multiply

their voices. And the child that walks among
them feels a muted wonder much like dread,
imagining how cold, and for how long,
she'd have to be to understand what's said.

Cracks

My dad tells me that he controls the weather.
"No, really," he insists when I begin
to laugh. And keeps insisting on it. When
at last belief encroaches on me—rather,
when doubt is tired and starting to wear thin—
he says it wasn't true. We laugh together.
I'm a little angry, though, by then.

Though it's a joke to him, some part of me
still sees him hefting lightning bolts, his hands
illumined, giving orders to the winds,
crafting a hurricane above the sea.
He looks away from his computer, stands
and walks into the kitchen, where his tea
is brewed and cooling. Casually he sends

a twister to the Midwest, adding sugar
to his cup, a touch of milk. He takes
it back to his home office, dropping flakes
of snow all down the hall. The storm grows bigger,
out of his control. A sea swell breaks.
He sits back down, familiar and transfigured.
A glacier fissures. California quakes.

Child Carrying a Dandelion

There's less of it with every step you take.
You shield the fluff that's left with your cupped hand
without success. You don't yet understand
the purpose of this fraying cumulus,
but if it took more than a breath to break
it into weightless tufts, you wouldn't fuss
to keep it whole. It isn't what you planned—
this galaxy of seeds loose in your wake.
You'd hoped to bring home something luminous.

A Grasshopper

The grasshopper is brittle, quick,
efficient as a lightning strike
and just as random. With a flick
of legs, it glances off a bike,
a hiker's arm, then back to mud
in sun-dried ruts. You don't expect
its heaviness, the little thud.
It hunkers down, brown, circumspect.

It clicks a little when it jumps,
then settles, stiff as well-starched lace.
In front of you, the cyclist bumps
along and mops his shining face.
You trudge uphill now, stepping on
a clump of grass, a rock, a root,
but not the grasshopper, who's gone
just when it should be underfoot.

Wide-Angle

The birds are taking back the power lines.
Huge flocks detach and dissipate, congeal
in pixelated darkening designs,
and settle single file. The sky, unreal

behind them, leaning over them, is green,
and they are backlit, black. A few adjust
their feathers. Watching through the window screen,
a child is thinking interstellar dust

might have a similar tendency to swirl
and sediment. Meanwhile, these dinosaurs
compose themselves, each tidy as a pearl,
and watch, from their high perch, our little wars.

The Fairy Path

Here the trees have faces: weary
eyes, cracked cheeks, a deepening scowl.
Hiking sounded good in theory
but you just heard something growl.

Company would have been better,
human company to keep
you insulated, like a sweater,
but your family is asleep.

So you're creeping up the trail,
touching lichen on a rock
as thoughtfully as you'd read Braille.
And the forest starts to talk.

"Come up higher!" insists the flicker
and the bright red columbine,
and your feet are moving quicker,
into thicker clumps of pine.

Animals emerge around you.
You can hear the distant creek
coming nearer, till the sound's too
loud to hear a person speak.

Deer and foxes watch intently.
They don't seem to find it weird
when you pause, and stretch, and gently
touch a pine tree's mossy beard.

Did you leave somebody sleeping?
Possibly, you can't recall,
and you also can't help leaping
right into the waterfall.

Visiting Switzerland at Seventeen

The window-boxes bleed geraniums.
The Alps smooth their kilometers of green.
Even the cows are bronze and burnished, straight
out of a fairy tale, and pretzel crumbs
taste better to the pigeons. Nonetheless,
people must be the same in any place:
they curse from bicycles, feel desolate
in church, get drunk. It seems as if they should
be constantly intoxicated by
the altitude, as if height might have bred
away the doubts under their fingernails,
the inner dinginess, the snow-capped lie.
But people are people, still, in fairy tales.

A Fairy Story

I. The Departure

At first she only wanders from the lane
a little way, remembering to bring back
the blackberries. The children have a snack.
She makes the cobbler, humming a refrain.

She scrubs her daughter's skirt—that berry stain
just won't come out. She thinks she hears her name
and shoves the window open. What a shame . . .
nobody's there. The floor grows slick with rain.

Next day she strays a little farther. Still,
she brings the berries home. Her children chase
the orange cat. Her husband says the grace.
She notices some lights atop the hill.

At dawn, she shuts the door without a sound.
Her blouse is thin. The sweater she forgot
is folded on a chair. The coffee pot
is boiling. Berries punctuate the ground.

II. The Return

She loathes the stench of iron and the sight
of every human face she used to love.
She spills the sugar in a figure eight
and leaves the burner glowing on the stove.

She hears hardly a word the children say
(her husband finds her talking with the cat)
and at her mother's grave she doesn't cry.
"What were you thinking?" "Dunno, I forget."

Her family are frightened of her now:
the angle of her head as she picks pears;
the brambles in her eyes; the way things grow
when she just looks at them (weeds, thistles, asters).

But she remembers sunsets like a bruise,
how everything was touched with wildness there,
and was itself, not tamed by common use.
The split ends fray to blossoms in her hair.

Mountain Wildflowers

Pale or gem-
toned they feed
the scant air,

love letters
tucked away
in plain sight.

Hikers come.
Loose rocks slide
here and there.

It matters
what you say
at this height.

Green People

Playfully we give them names like Gregor,
Ferdinand, but marvel at ringed flesh,
at rivered cheeks, the staidness of their vigor,
the dull jade of a flickering eyelash,

wondering—have we disrespected dryads
with our jokes? Slim aspens, earrings flashing,
the maudlin willow with her tattered braids,
the laugh-lined ponderosa, always blushing,

repeat their own pet names for humans over
a brunch of sunlight, cheerfully complaining
of letters scratched in bark. One sips the river
and remarks, "How hot it's been." Well-meaning

though that comment was, it's changed the mood,
for suddenly there's talk of thirst and beetles.
"Did you see her burns?" one whispers. "How could
she survive it?" And their dry breath rattles.

An Apprehension

Something is approaching languidly
through grasses which the sun has made its own.
Their white tongues stiffen, hiss. A lone
bird, startled, startles me.

I came this way, I can't remember why.
Maybe I had a choice, or maybe not.
The bird, flapping away, is caught
by an unflinching sky.

A ripple, not quite shadow, parts the grass
here, there, a shivered whisper in the heat.
The ripple pauses at my feet
and will not pass.

Inventory of a Shop in Berkeley

Colored trinkets. Tiny dolls.
Sugar spoons and paper balls.

Queen sized bed. Handmade lace.
Clock with an astonished face.

Spices. Perfumes. Bottled ciders.
Mossy branches. Cobwebs. Spiders.

Songbirds twittering in cages.
Spell-book missing half its pages.

Roosters with real feathers. Sunlight.
Silver mirror, scarcely child-height.

Wooden table made by Shakers.
Silence spread in dusty acres.

Woman, vast, with cobweb hair,
permanently in her chair.

Quilted coat of many colors.
"You can have it for five dollars."

Rumbling laughter. Needle threaded
with a camel. Dog, three-headed.

Fragile vase of baby's breath.
Fraying twine. A family death.

The Drive

The car labored up vertical streets, imperiled
by each red light or stop sign, and I, dreaming
against the window, saw a manhole steaming—
an obvious entrance to the underworld.

I sat up straighter, sure that Cerberus
was more than those three yapping dogs being walked
beyond the chain link fence. My mother locked
the doors—this part of town was dangerous.

If I had been Persephone I would
have uprooted a scraggly dandelion
from a sidewalk crack, and Hades, drawn
by neighing shadows, and in love with childhood,

would have sprung up from that hole—the reason
why she locked the doors was something like that.
She drove on, past a dirty laundromat.
I rolled my window down to let the breeze in

and whatever our actual destination was
makes no real difference now—the steam is only
steam, and Hades isn't very lonely,
and I'm the one who locks the doors because.

Childproofing

She covered up the stars in case they burned.
She locked up politics, religion, sex,
well out of reach, but every time she turned
around, she was confronted with bright flecks

of controversy in the carpet or
her daughter's hair. Diluted cruelties
soaked through the ceiling, seeped up from the floor.
The daughter, meanwhile, petted bumblebees,

provoked lightning to fork, stepped on the cracks
in grownup logic, squirreled away old dead-
bolts in her yellow skirt, sighed, "Mom, relax,"
when bullets grazed the window by her bed.

Sticks

Even this denuded schoolyard has one:
good for whacking signposts, poking treetops,
skewering the eyeball of a cyclops,
building fires. It's never out of season,

a good stick. The sound it makes when breaking
satisfies you, how the struck end splinters
sharply into stardust—an enchanter's
staff. You flourish it a little, speaking

languages revealed to children only,
and it flowers into rose and lilac.
Try to stuff it, somehow, in your backpack;
it resists, as magic does. You'll soon be

home and it will be your mother screeching
"Put that stick away!" across the yard, and
"Want to keep both eyes?" while you skim quicksand,
vault past giants, give the sun a thrashing.

Fiber Arts

It all seems innocent enough.
They have a loom, a spinning wheel,
and baskets blooming with brown fluff,
which you're invited, now, to feel.

There's no need for suspicion, surely.
They have gentle faces. But
it doesn't matter how demurely
they hold scissors—those things cut.

The oldest woman wields a hook.
Her feet are planted on the rug
with an abyss between them. "Look,"
she croaks, giving the yarn a tug.

You stay to watch the wool transform,
its lone dimension turned to two—
a thread grown complicated, warm,
compelling—and she grins at you.

"Here, hold this," while she snips the end.
Two blades shiver apart, then join
with one chill note. Smile back, pretend
you didn't hear; no bitter coin

is hidden underneath your tongue.
You turn away, intent on leaving.
Then another woman, young
and rounded, rises from her weaving.

Something tangles in your gut.
Panic. Blunder towards the door.
(Later you will wonder what
all that hysteria was for.)

STAT

A life can't be composed of urgencies
like that—the sound the broken ambulance
made as you prayed inside it—how, by chance,
it got you safely there—electric skies

flattened against the window of the room
where the Bulgarian night nurse told you to
get up and walk—the stench of soap—the blue
curtain dividing you from your own womb—

and someone crying—and his damp black hair
under your hand (but that was later, hours
went by before you saw him, sprouting wires
like bristles on a porcupine). It's fair

to say you wouldn't want your life to be
like that, although a crisis here or there
is bearable and useful. "Now take care,"
they say as they discharge you. Urgency

moves its attention, and your life assumes
a plainer aspect, and the laundry waits,
though nothing you can do alleviates
the strangeness of that ambulance, those rooms.

Reading Skin

Through the little glass he squints,
into a geography
of moles and scars. He doesn't see
the telltale mark. Mortality
has not left any fingerprints.

In her open gown, she shifts
uneasily. The room is cold.
The doctor checks inside a fold
of flesh. Still waiting to be told
that everything is fine, she lifts

one arm and then the other, turns
her back when asked, and hopes her skin
won't give too much away (the thin
pink seam across her abdomen,
the bumps and bruises). "No concerns

for now," he says. "Come back next year."
She puts her clothes back on and walks
into the sun. A red-tailed hawk's
rehearsing circles, and the clocks
are twitching, and she has a queer

feeling of someone drawing near,
some hooded figure from the past
perhaps, a bleached iconoclast,
implacable, approaching fast,
and babbling like an auctioneer.

Without a Pause

Time stomps downstairs
in his yellow suit,
his hair gone silver
at the root.

"Now, won't you have
some tea?" I say.
He waves a hand—
he mustn't stay,

his feet are lead,
they drag him on
as steadily
as coaches drawn

by an old nag
whose face is turned
away from something
small and burned.

"All right, goodbye,"
I'd like to say.
Instead I trail him
through decay,

trying to marvel
at winking dust,
the smell of moss,
the taste of rust.

Fall

Two men, one woman stamp across the street
in faded coats. Cars elbow past. The sky
is metal gray, and low, as if the weight
of human misery held it. With a sigh

the wind stands up. A wash of gold unravels
across the road, the sidewalk, people, cars.
The city is submerged in pale gold ovals.
The small group turns a corner, shedding stars.

Out of Proportion

All winter a giantess watched us from the horizon,
tapping her fingers Fee-Fi-Fo-Fum on the road.
"It's only traffic," we said in the voice of reason,
"and the sun shining through a tree." We were scared; it showed.

We were driving home when she leaned in close to the window,
her hair a confusion of branches in silhouette,
and half the world dropped into sudden shadow
as her breath emboldened the end of her cigarette.

She didn't touch the car, only startled a rabbit
from the tangled underbrush as we whisked by,
and I thought she spoke—but that might have been my heartbeat,
out of breath and knocking on the sky.

Giants Crossing

"Watch for giants," says the sign,
as if by watching one could do
anything effective to
avoid being crushed. Is it benign,

this warning? On a lovely day
suppose some great foot flattens you;
would it be helpful if you knew
beforehand? Would you stop to pray

instead of taking in the view?
Or would you merely agonize
until the moment of demise?
Better it comes out of the blue.

Of course, the giants don't intend
to trample us. They're passing through,
they really haven't got a clue
we're here. And since we cannot fend

them off by observation, why
make signs? Try to forget that you
live in the shadow of a shoe
whose owner's merely passing by.

A Barbary Lion

The lion elegantly tucks his paw
beneath his chin, considering his prey.
He doesn't know he's red in tooth and claw
or why this dinner fails to run away

but finds the scene compelling, truth be told.
He'd find it somewhat less so if he knew
he was symbolic, just a show of gold
brought out for everyone to misconstrue.

But he can't help his lack of metaphor,
the physicality of sinews, teeth,
and fur. He doesn't suddenly grow more
carnivorous before a laurel wreath.

He doesn't care that it's his privilege
to feast on saints—these animals who stand
impatiently at the illumined edge
of being. He stretches, walks across the sand,

and hesitates. Their willingness to die
does not entice him. When at length he bites
an arm off, and then mutilates an eye,
it's simple hunger, and his appetite's

not quite sufficient for the whole affair.
He's prodded with a spear, to no avail.
Saints lie half-martyred, but he doesn't care—
the lion walks away, flicking his tail.

Limbo

The cottonwoods were snowing on the day
the sun went out. We guessed, at first, eclipse—
then, when the darkness stayed, apocalypse—
but learned to breathe in that unearthly gray

(yes, gray, because there *was* still light, although
nobody could identify its source)
for lack of other options. And of course
the wind continued, casually, to blow

the cotton from the branches to the grass.
We wandered through pale rapids, trampled pools
and eddies of its fleece. We looked like ghouls
in search of graves—but whether to harass

the occupants or to lie down ourselves
in quiet rectangles, we couldn't tell.
And whether that serenely tolling bell
was meant for us, our smoldering bookshelves

would not disclose, nor whether this was Hell.

The Leaf Blower

He makes the wind do what it's told.
Well, not exactly; wind resists,
but he gets paid to use his fists.
In this world nature's bought and sold
and blown around haphazardly.
He walks below each storm-shorn tree,
stomping through drifts of leafy mold,
swinging his gadget side to side.
He won't ask why, won't break his stride,
just breezily redistributes gold.

Bigfoot

Of course she knows what humans are.
Their lights that cloud all but the brightest star
warn her away. And from afar

she watches them pollute the streams,
burn trees, drill, detonate. Sometimes in dreams
she follows them. The landscape seems

to die a little where they walk,
as if their lightest footsteps hollowed rock.
In dreams she understands their talk

but can't assemble, when she wakes,
the shreds of meaning that their babble makes.
She lies unmoving till day breaks;

at last, with a soft groan, she stirs
and stamps about among the conifers.
If she avoids their world, will hers

be left alone, her woodland haunt
untouched? Solitude draws them like a taunt.
It isn't even what they want

but what they know that they can take.
New snow floats down. She blinks away a flake.
The silence settles like an ache.

Unbecoming

Wild mushrooms glowing insolently white.
Insistent pebbles. Unrepentant ferns.
Only the human tortuously learns
to keep her rougher edges out of sight.

Until she can't. She finds herself composed
entirely of elbows, odor, waste.
Her fellows turn away; they feel debased
by what they've seen. She knocks; the doors are closed.

She'd thought that she was made of gauzier stuff.
Meandering vaguely towards the still-vague dawn,
she finds some mushrooms glowing in a lawn—
irregular, unwelcome, real enough.

Things Done and Left Undone

The sun is low,
the shadows tinged

with flies. Someone
has come unhinged;

across the lawn
we hear him shout

profanities.
Then he comes out.

He's swearing at
another man

who backs away
towards a sedan.

The first man hits
the second. We

are silent. From
a balcony

one woman yells,
then disappears.

Our game has stopped.
The courtyard clears.

"Let's go," a boy
softly insists.

We leave the man
to his friend's fists,

to hot cement
and creeping dark.

A tiny dog
begins to bark.

With the Current

Bare-armed, gargantuan, he paces near
the traffic, dips a toe from time to time
into the constant stream of other lives,
then draws it back. The mythic feeds and thrives
on such proportions; he would be sublime
in someone else's story. But he's here,

pacing and muttering to himself, on edge.
Two dozen lives flow briskly past. He moves
away a little, stamping through a drift
of snow. I feel my own attention shift,
already reaching past him into grooves
as deeply worn as his. I pass the hedge,

I pass him, as I did just yesterday
and might tomorrow, but for now he's gone,
diminished in my mirror. Possibly
he'll wander underneath that willow tree
into a better story. I drive on,
skimming past lives I can't touch anyway.

For a Neighbor

It's 8 p.m. and there's that song again.
Always the same one, or it sounds the same
to me. I can distinguish the refrain
by how the walls respond. The slapdash frame

of the apartment building might collapse.
You wouldn't mind. In fact the way your bones
test their own limits thrills you. And perhaps
it's philosophical—the undertones

suggesting that we're all just being taken
for a ride, that life essentially
consists of shaking others and being shaken
harder: rhythm without melody.

Renovation

Our landlord's busy touching up the sky
with dabs of blue, a little marbled white.
Birds dart from hollow walls when he walks by,
but never mind—he's busy with the sky,
he really can't be bothered to ask why
there's water dripping from the hallway light.
He straightens out a corner of the sky
and mutters, "If you want something done right . . ."

Old Cars

She knows he doesn't think about her much.
His touch
is not particularly tender.
That time her fender
bent,
there was no evident
remorse.
Her paint's a mess and only getting worse.

And yet he needs her. They are both aware
of her utility. He may not care
beyond
his need, may not be fond
of her, exactly, but
each morning when her door slams shut
he prays
that everything keeps running for a few more days
or even just today, and surely
that is love, she thinks obscurely.

Harpies

I understand her better now, the neighbor
screeching "Anne!" in her corroded voice.
Her preteen daughter had to make a choice:
follow that cry (a kind of mythic labor)

or keep on running, covering her ears.
(A mother can be tiresome, it's true.
She flaps about. She tells you what to do.
You want to ride the wind; she interferes.)

I flex my claws. Now I'm the one who shrieks
my son's name rustily through the neighborhood.
"Come home!" But calling doesn't do much good;
the kids are weary of our wings and beaks.

The Bath

The tub's a satin animal with claws,
gulping down hollowness. I climb in, slide

my spine along its slope. The rising tide
finds incandescence where the moon once was.

I start to drift. The sea is porcelain.
The seabirds hover, holding back their cries.

Clouds blind the mirror. I reorganize
my nakedness, breaking the water's pane

with knees and elbows into pointed waves,
into a world of angles, smooth and steep.

Hold still. How white the water goes, how deep.
Humiliations surface like old graves;

pale childhood laps my chin. And yet I know
that simply getting out will break the spell.

The foam disperses: this is a hotel,
and I stopped playing mermaid years ago.

Poem Illuminated by a Crow

The boy comes in, his limp hair starred with snow,
in tears because a neighbor wouldn't play
his game. The window's dark. A single crow
struts on a plane of white. What should you say,

should you console him, tell him it's no loss?
Or that a life grows bright with losses, ripe
to splitting with them? Tell him it's a toss-
up whether this one matters. Time will wipe

away its sting, or else he'll sit up sweating
in the middle of the night for years,
remembering the neighbor's face, forgetting
that there was a crow. You dry his tears.

Sanctuary

Then he longed for someone vast to wrap
    him in sunset, hold
him, steady him on her iron lap
    in a drizzle of gold

that would shade his face like a woman's hair.
    A childish thought.
Of course he would bear what he could bear
    and what he could not,

and would bear it alone. He didn't pray
    (with his tongue gone raw)
that the cup that was his might be taken away,
    but looked up and saw

the roofs of houses flattening
    as the sun went down
and the golf course netting rigged like wings
    above the town.

Knitting Lesson

My grandmother is teaching me to knit
again. Her hands, though mostly ash, are warm
and practiced. My own stitches twist and split
and argue, always failing to conform.

She's not disheartened by my efforts. She
inspects the sorry scarf, transforming it
by her appraisal. "Nobody will see
that from a galloping horse,"—she fibs a bit.

She knows the alchemy of error, how
a dropped stitch may become a buttonhole.
Mistakes can be repurposed, even now.
No matter how you tangle up the wool

it can be wound again, a life's loose ends
be woven in—or that's the hope we live in.
She folds the crooked cloth into my hands
and crumbles into memory, forgiven.

Inspiration

Wind beneath
my sweater, wind
embezzling breath.
Sky-handled, skinned

by cloudlessness,
I can't recall
a feeling less
ethereal

than this. I walk
past plundered trees.
Wind raids my pockets,
bares my knees.

I smooth down my
exterior
but the wind cries,
tries even more

to rearrange
me in its paws,
and leaves me stranger
than I was.

Adamantine

She builds her sonnets to resist
the elements of pain and doubt,
turning each sentence inside out
to look for holes she might have missed
and tightening the rhymes, which twist
to get away. Her octaves shout
their dissidence. Her sestets pout.
She rules them with an iron fist.

But in her dreams the poems drift,
anarchic, in a shipwreck's wake.
She touches one and finds it soft
as skin and almost as opaque.
She thinks, *There will be nothing left—
like skin, they're liable to break.*

Her Broad-Brimmed Hat

protects her from the sun and people's eyes.
Yes, strangers, but especially those she knows.
She puts it on: she may be brutal, wise
or witty, it won't matter. Nothing shows.

She wears its shadow at a slant. She tells
her friends that she's allergic to the light.
Perhaps they have their own straw citadels
arranged just so. Perhaps an anchorite

inhabits each of them as well—or not.
She smiles from underneath the tilted weave,
and visits the adjoining room, where thought
is cloistered. "Shy," they mutter, "odd, naive."

Reading Hart Crane in the School Parking Lot

Pines drop unsteady patterns on the page.
Even with the windows down, it's hot.
I'm trying to find meaning in an image:
"the leopard in the brow." The meaning's caught

on something—an eye socket or incisor.
The shadows on the paper flower like beads
in a kaleidoscope and then resolve.
The leopard wanders off. I, none the wiser,

turn a page. Two severed heads float past;
perhaps the leopard's exodus proved fatal.
A car radio babbles, and the breeze
brings in exhaust. The shadows of the trees

grow hazy, flicker, pass over the words
like hands half-covering a face. It's three
o'clock: school's getting out. I leave my car
locked up with Crane's inscrutability.

A Few Minor Poets

They've come together just to stand
a little ways apart, the pear
trees blossoming between them and
restraint electric in the air.

They won't apologize—cannot—
for what is small and polished, for
meticulously tended plots
of weeds, for wanting to explore

an unused corner of a drawer
in someone's dresser. No one else
wanted the day-old apple core,
the seahorse on the carousel.

The sun is going down. They drift
among the petals and the leaves,
scribbling, with customary thrift,
their own familiar leitmotifs,

and none of them is interested
in what a minor poet is,
being busy with that shade of red
that brands the hem of the abyss.

The Muse

She's in the bathroom coloring her face.
"Please come," I say. She laughs, won't turn around,
her creams and powders all over the place,
her shoulders stooped a little and sun-browned.

The others aren't persuaded by her poses
(hair arranged just so, expression grave).
She turns her head a little and discloses
a hint of serpent, profile of a wave.

They ridicule. She hides a streak of glitter
on her cheekbone, tints it skin-toned, matte.
I marvel at her—how she won't grow bitter.
She stands up, and there's stardust where she sat.

"Where do you want to go?" I ask. And now
she faces me, and all the paint can't hide
the comet in the angle of her eyebrow,
the turquoise of her forehead, many-eyed.

She pauses to secure a straying twist
of wind behind her ear. She smooths a cloud.
"Come on," she says, and grins and grabs my wrist.
We walk anonymously through the crowd.

Figure Drawing

"Don't breathe," he says.
Your shadow stays

taped round once more
on chair and floor.

The heater purrs.
The blank wall blurs.

You shift your weight.
The buzzer's late.

The clock is slow.
The skylight glows

with bouncing hail.
Your muscles feel

pain creeping in.
What's real grows thin.

What hurts grows bright
and still and slight.

A voice calls "Break!"
Your muscles ache.

Your robe is warm
obscuring form.

The Female Form

Finding some paintings by Magritte—
in which, dissected by his mind,
nude women fracture and repeat,

or fish with female legs, consigned
to helpless flopping on the shore,
stare glassy-eyed—to be unkind

and too disturbing to ignore,
I closed the book and made it stay
beneath some clothing in a drawer,

forgotten. But I think today
of Meng—whose bones, fantastically,
having been crushed (some versions say)

and then discarded in the sea,
swam off, all silver. And before
I know it, fractured women free

themselves, collecting from the floor
neglected body parts, pale knees
and faces. Glassy-eyed no more,

the woman-fish compels a breeze
to roll her back among the waves,
with no one but herself to please.

No one stops them. No one saves
them. Someone runs to tell Magritte
his paint dislocates, misbehaves.

The women find that they have feet,
and thoughts, and names. To his dismay
they drop their frames and walk away,
inviolate, shining, down the street.

Faux Pas

She showed up to the party with a goat.
That was the first offense; the second was
a lengthy, convoluted anecdote;
the third, the way she'd tilt her head and pause

mid-sentence; fourth, and unforgivable,
a preference (unconcealed) for being alone.
She'd fade into the wallpaper. They'd pull
her back to their reality—flesh tones,

first names, locked faces—and she'd float up toward
the ceiling. Laboring to close her hand
around a glass of wine, they held her, bored
her with their gossip, made her understand

that floating was improbable. Her skin
became evasive as an alley-cat.
The goat began to play the violin.
She fed him shriveled rosebuds from her hat.

The Opposite of Aging

Even as a child she has some
heaviness about her eyes,
which makes sorrowers feel welcome,
which convinces them she's wise.

So the grownups tell her secrets,
truths too big for her to carry,
and she listens to each grievance
calmly, without commentary.

Quietly she walks, bent double,
hobbles down the crowded hall
where her classmates' clear untroubled
laughter rings out like a bell.

Quietly she buys a white dress,
quietly becomes a mother.
Quietly she shifts her secrets
from one hip bone to the other

and although she's growing older
something new is happening,
some new straightness in her shoulders,
brand-new glinting hint of wing.

One chill morning, newly widowed,
she gets up, her hair gone gray,
quietly unlocks the window,
swallows grief, and floats away.

On Rising

The dead man tries to gather up his grave
but fumbles it. Loose linen cloths unroll.
The earthworms munching tunnels through his soul
disperse. The daffodils he hopes to save—

collecting yellow armfuls—bleach and fade.
The dirt under his nails has grown abstract.
At last he wanders through a star, hunchbacked
and naked, half convinced he might have stayed.

In the Giants' Cottage

The giants' home is vast, well-lit.
Although its size disorients at first,
the contents are conventional:
the window where the giants like to sit,
the lamps and tables interspersed
with pots of flowers, the landscapes on the wall.

It's a peculiar place to be
after your time below; they know you're here
and treat you as their special guest.
Each afternoon the giantess serves tea
with sandwiches. Her cats appear
and rub against your chair. You're not distressed

by their immensity, you're quite
untroubled here, except when you recall
small horrors from your past, but that's
all over, you remember you're all right.
Your hosts are warm and genial.
You stroke the fur of the enormous cats.

How serious disaster seemed
back then! The bodies no one dared retrieve,
genocide, atom bombs. And how
you longed for something like this cottage, dreamed
of peace you couldn't quite believe.
But everything is in perspective now . . .

Emily and Blake

She pokes and prods eternity,
the method flowering in her hand.
He stares his seraphs into being,
strides over fire and stokes the wind.

But do their Heavens intersect?
Suppose they do. Suppose she sweeps
her snow across the ruby floor
and startles tigers from the drapes.

He locates deity in her face.
She turns away, adjusts her shawl,
and prunes the void a bit. He puts
the trimmings out to brighten Hell.

For Sergei Prokofiev

Words are a blunt instrument
for this harmonic swagger, dissonant
euphoria, the way
even your deadly seriousness turns to play.

You limp along a bit, then all at once
seize in a dance
the Grim Reaper, whose recessed face betrays alarm
at the frenzy of your fingers on his arm.

I can imagine
you taking my arm in a similar fashion,
as violet graves and turquoise shadows stagger by
kaleidoscopically.

A Dream

My aunt's ghost walks in silence through the house,
touching a painting here, a curtain there,
evaluating beading on a blouse.

We talk a little, all the while aware
that she is present, absent. Is her gaze
benevolent? Does she no longer care?

She passes through the kitchen, spilling sprays
of flowers—lilies—burgundy and blue.
Too many to be crammed into a vase.

And then my dad's parents show up. They, too,
are ghosts. My grandmother surveys the scene,
the uncooked food, the photographs askew.

My grandfather, as usual, is keen
to get a photo of us as a group,
to frame some harmony that might have been.

I perch uncomfortably on the stoop
out front, among the wooden elephants.
My cousins crowd around, a lively troupe.

I sing a dirge. They look at me askance.
I read psalms from the Book of Common Prayer.
"Be still," I read. My aunt begins to dance.

Assisting the Day

Rain fumbling with an elegy, and rain
meandering down the windowpane,
waking me underwater.
The day begins to totter
up the lane,
wearing her thin fringed shawl again.

I take her arm. Each puddle is a stain
of sun. The gutter's a bright vein,
and snails are scribbling
silver notes. The day walks slowly, dribbling
yarrow and fleabane
all down the front of her terrain.

She pauses, toying with a weather vane.
I try to ascertain
whether she needs to rest,
but, though she's only nominally dressed
and feels, she says, a certain strain,
the day will not lie down, does not complain.

Mildred

I didn't want to sing. The venue was
unsettling—her muffled figure crying
in bed in a white building where the dying
went to be bewildered. But because

I wanted to be kind, I held her veined
translucent hand—substantial, still, but barely—
knowing my unease was temporary.
As was hers, but with a different end.

So. "Good King Wenceslas" and "We Three Kings"
and the angelic host. She listened, grieving
loss, or kindness—or perhaps believing
that her daughter stood there, wearing wings.

After Hail

Stones are melting in the grass,
the size of marbles, little globes
pale and opaque as frosted glass
that shiver when my finger probes
    them. Everywhere I pass

I see the wreckage of the storm:
the broken branch, the dented car,
the flowers it labored to deform.
I don't dare venture very far
    in case another swarm

of miniature worlds should sting
my skin. I wander through the yard
where galaxies lie glittering
in sudden sun. The ground is scarred
    with light and everything

drips quietly. After the flood
were birds so still, the sky so bright?
I pause to save an injured bud
then walk across the dirty white
    of petals crushed in mud.

Puddle Gazing

The pothole's filled with water, and a child
is crouched devoutly over it, the rest
of life shut out, her pink windbreaker pulled
over her head. The rain is falling fast

and fine; the light is hesitant behind
thin cloud cover. Her contemplation deepens,
driving past the ripples to the ground,
immaculately black. Here nothing happens,

down here nothing stirs that she can see,
not even dirt. It looks as if this hole
might swallow her, since already the sky
has fallen in, pale and improbable

and dizzying and clarifying. Then
a name rings out. The jacket slips. Her head
is bare and sequined suddenly with rain.
She jumps over the puddle, runs inside.

Nestlings

Imagine being born up high, aware
first of a blur
of blossoms. Your whole nursery
is wallpapered with sky.

The winds are cold,
unsettling, but petaled
spaciousness is all you know.
The bough

tends constantly to bend
and sway. The ground
is theoretical, an unreal rumor of solidity;
that heady

drop is just one distance among
distances. Your mother's song
stops when you ask her what "down" means.
She flies away. Then come the rains,

blown at sharp angles to your nest.
Each gust
feels like a loss—you learn
to worry that she won't return.

But just as suddenly, it stops. The sun
appears again:
pale, powerless, but lovely. And she's back,
a white worm in her beak.

First Fishing Trip

You've hoped to bring him here
    since infancy,
to this hole in the river
where the fish are sure to hide.
So here we are, outside.
    You cast. I shiver
underneath a dripping tree.
The fish do not appear.

It isn't quite the trip
    you had in mind:
our car stuck in the snow,
the line forever in a knot.
At least we're at the spot
    you picked, although
it took a few attempts to find.
I'm worried that you'll slip

or that the ice will crack,
    the river flood.
My seat is damp. I meant
to bring a book but I forgot.
It's getting almost hot—
    by accident
I throw your jacket in the mud.
I guess it's good it's black.

Still, no one's lost a limb.
    It's nice: fresh air,
the bracing smell of pine.
Nothing has bitten yet, but you're
trying a different lure,
    untangling line
again. "Lower your voice, don't scare
the fish," you caution him.

And now the only sound
    comes from pine branches
loudly unburdening
themselves of melting snow. And birds.
I dare to glance upwards.
    Above me, something
pops and little avalanches
fall. It feels profound.

About the Author

Hilary Biehl grew up in California but has lived much of her life in New Mexico. She is a graduate of St. John's College in Santa Fe, where she studied the Western classics. Her poems have appeared in various journals, including *Able Muse, Mezzo Cammin, Blue Unicorn, THINK, The Orchards Poetry Journal,* and *The Lyric.*

www.ingramcontent.com/pod-product-compliance
Lightning Source LLC
Chambersburg PA
CBHW030912170426
43193CB00009BA/821